<u>Recipes of the Italian cuisine</u>

NONNA MARIA

Table of contents

Pasta, risotto & Co.

Risotto nero with squid
Risotto with truffle
Penne with spicy sauce
spaghetti carbonara
spaghetti bolognese
Tagliatelle with saffron sauce
rigatoni al pesto
Ravioli with spinach and sage butter
Cannelloni with tomato & mozzarella filling

Pizza & Baked Goods

capricciosa pizza
Pizza with mussels
Pizza Calzone with meat filling
focaccia alla romana
Calabrese
Pizza frutti di mare

Fleisch und Geflügel

Chicken pan piquant and spicy
Roast pork in milk
Rabbit with tomatoes and herbs
Schnitzel with Marsala sauce
Roast beef in Barolo
Stuffed fillet of beef Lombard style
Stuffed veal breast Ligurian style
Lamb stew with mushrooms

Fish and seafood

Sole fillets au gratin
Sea bass with olive sauce
Red mullets with pancetta
Grilled tuna with anchovies
Stuffed trout with crayfish tails
Swordfish in Marsala
Fried prawns Venetian style
Stuffed mussels with tomatoes
Stuffed squid with potatoes
Gilthead seabream with onions

Dolci

Cream puffs to fill
Figs stuffed with chocolate
Tiramisù
Panforte Tuscan fruit cake
Panna Cotta with Marsala and mint
Lemon cake light and fresh
Zabaione with Marsala and lemon
Cantuccini Tuscan style
Melon sorbet Sicilian style
Ricotta ice cream with espresso
Amaretto parfait with figs

Foreword

Dall'antipasto al dolce...
In Italy, food is not just a simple intake of food. It's
connectedness, it's joy of life, it's a true passion. When you
eat for the first time in Italy - whether in a trattoria, an
osteria or at a friend's house - it will be difficult to control
yourself. The aromas, the feelings of happiness, la dolce vita.
You won't be able to stop eating.
But what makes this cuisine one of the most popular in the
world? Is it because of the people, the ingredients or the
exceptionally good preparation? Or do all these factors
perhaps play a role?

Mediterranean cuisine lives from the freshness of its herbs,
the best olive oil, sun-ripened fruits and vegetables and
unique pasta dishes.
Through this book you will learn and taste step by step that
Italy has so much more to offer.

Welcome to Italy...

Antipasti & Soups

Beef carpaccio

For 4 servings:
Salt
Pepper
300g fillet of beef
fat and sinewless
1 celery
2 tablespoons lemon juice
5 tablespoons olive oil
50g parmesan or
Grana Padano

1. Put the fillet of beef in the freezer for about 1 hour Then cut into thin slices.
Wash and finely dice the

2. perennial celery. Mix lemon juice with oil and salt.

3. place the fillet slices on a plate and season with freshly ground pepper. Then add the lemon-oil mixture.

4. let the whole thing stand for 30 minutes and cover with foil. Finally add the cheese and the celery cubes.

Preparation time: about 20 minutes
Per portion approx. 260 kcal/1092 kJ
19 g E, 19 g F, 2 g KH

Bruschetta with tomatoes

For 4 servings:
Salt
Pepper
2 cloves of garlic
2 beef tomatoes
1/2 bunch basil
1 baguette
5-6 tbsp olive oil

1. preheat oven grill to 200 °C . Peel the garlic cloves. Wash the beef tomatoes and cut into small cubes.

2. season tomato cubes with salt and pepper Wash and dry the basil and cut the leaves into small cubes. Then mix the basil with the diced tomatoes.

3.slice the baguette and bake in the oven until crispy and golden brown. Then rub them well with the garlic cloves before spreading the olive oil and tomato sauce over them.

Preparation time: about 20 minutes
Per portion approx. 178 kcal/749 kJ
3 g E, 10 g F, 20 g KH

Parma ham with melon

For 4 servings:
Salt
Pepper
1 honeydew melon
130 g Parma ham
in thin slices
2 tomatoes
1/2 bunch flat parsley
1/2 bunch basil
100 ml olive oil
50 ml wine vinegar

1. cut the melon in half, remove the seeds and cut into slices. Arrange melon and ham slices decoratively on plates.

2. briefly scalding tomatoes in hot water, then peeling and finely dicing them. Wash, dry and chop the herbs.

3.mix olive oil with vinegar, tomatoes and herbs to a marinade. Add salt and pepper to taste.

4.drip marinade over the ham. Buon appetito!

Preparation time: approx. 30 minutes
Per portion approx. 347 kcal/1459 kJ
18 g E, 38 g F, 5 g KH

Zucchini - cream soup

The preparation:
For 4 servings
Salt
Pepper
550 g zucchini
1 onion
1 garlic clove
1/4 tsp cayenne pepper
2 tablespoons olive oil
600 ml vegetable broth
40 ml dry white wine
150 g cream
2 tablespoons basil leaves

1. clean and chop the zucchini Peel and finely chop the onion and garlic. Heat the oil in a pot and fry the onions first. Then add garlic and zucchini. Steam for about 3 minutes while stirring.

2.now add broth and season with salt and pepper. Simmer covered for about 20 minutes. Refine with cream and wine, bring to the boil and puree the soup.

3.wash the basil leaves and cut into small strips. Arrange the soup on the plates and decorate with basil.

Preparation time
Approx. 25 minutes & cooking time
Per serving
Approx. 310 kcal/1300 kJ
8 g E, 23 g F, 19 g KH

Minestrone

The preparation
For 4 portions
50 g fresh broad beans (without pods)
50 g belly bacon
175 g fresh peas (without pods)
200 g carrots, 200 g zucchini, 200 g potatoes
1/2 onion
1 stick of leek
1 stick of celery
200 g savoy cabbage
200 g rice
250 g peeled tomatoes
3 tablespoons butter
1 garlic clove
1 tablespoon chopped parsley
1 tablespoon chopped oregano
Freshly sliced Parmesan cheese
Salt

1. wash and chop the vegetables. Then cut potatoes, onions, savoy cabbage and bacon into small cubes. Instead, cut the leek into rings.

2.heat butter in a big pot and add bacon cubes first, then onion and leek. Steam the whole thing for a few minutes. Add remaining vegetables with liquid. Season everything with salt and pepper and simmer for about 5 minutes.

Add 3.2 L water, bring to the boil and simmer covered for about 45 minutes. Bring the soup to the boil and stir in the rice. Let it simmer until rice is ready. Peel garlic, chop finely and add. Spread minestrone on the plates and sprinkle with herbs and sliced Parmesan cheese.

Preparation time
Approx. 50 minutes & cooking time
Per serving
Approximately 725 kcal/3040 kJ
16 g E, 44 g F, 62 g KH

Tomato soup

The preparation:
For 4 servings
1 pinch of sugar
Salt
800 g ripe tomatoes
2 onions
2 tablespoons grappa
2 tablespoons butter
250 ml vegetable broth
4 tablespoons cream
1 handful of basil leaves

1.cut tomatoes, blanch hot, remove seeds and cut into small pieces. Peel and chop the onions.

2. melt butter in a pot and fry onions in it. Add the tomatoes and braise for about 30 minutes at medium temperature, stirring several times, until a puree is formed.

3.fill up with the stock and puree in a blender. Bring the soup to the boil in the pot, season with sugar, salt and grappa.

4.whip the cream until stiff, wash the basil and cut into fine strips. Put the tomato soup on plates, garnish with some cream and basil.

Preparation time
Approx. 30 minutes & cooking time
Per serving
Approx. 250 kcal/1060 kJ
4 g E, 21 g F, 11 g KH

Vegetables & Salads

Tomatoes spicy filled

The preparation:
For 4 servings
4 medium sized tomatoes
50 g breadcrumbs
2 cloves of garlic
1 bunch of flat parsley
8 tablespoons freshly grated
Parmesan

1. preheat the oven to 200 °C (convection oven). Wash and halve the tomatoes and hollow them out with a spoon. Drain the tomato halves in a sieve.

2.peel garlic and chop finely. Then wash and chop the parsley.

3.mix breadcrumbs with 6 tbsp. oil, garlic and parsley. Season with salt and pepper.

4.put this filling into the tomato halves and sprinkle the cheese on top. Grease the baking tray with oil. Put the tomato halves on top and bake in the oven for about 30 minutes. Perfect side dish with meat or fish.

Preparation time
Approx. 25 minutes & baking time
Per serving
Approx. 397 kcal/1670 kJ
23 g E, 29 g F, 13 g KH

Baked zucchini

The preparation
For 4 portions
4 courgettes
salt, pepper
2 shallots
2 garlic clove
2 tablespoons flour
2 tablespoons breadcrumbs
2 tablespoons freshly grated
Pecorino
4 tablespoons olive oil
1 handful of fresh mint
1 bunch of flat parsley
400 g tomatoes
Juice of 1 lemon

1. preheat the oven to 200 °C Peel, wash and slice the zucchini. Peel and finely chop the shallots and garlic.

2. put flour in a bowl and turn the zucchini slices in it. Heat some oil in a frying pan and fry the zucchini slices until golden brown. Then take them out and put them aside.

3. wash the herbs and chop them finely. Put the rest of the oil in the pan and fry the shallots, garlic, tomatoes with juice and herbs (only half of the parsley). After about 3 minutes, spice vigorously with salt and pepper and remove the pan from the heat.

4.grease the casserole dish. Add half of the zucchini slices and sprinkle with some lemon juice. Pour the pan mixture over them and then place the remaining zucchini slices on top. Add the rest of the lemon juice.

5.sprinkle breadcrumbs and cheese mixture over the vegetables. Bake in the oven for about 20 minutes. Sprinkle with remaining parsley and serve.

Preparation time

Approx. 30 minutes & baking time

Per serving

Approx. 293 kcal/1230 kJ

9 g E, 17 g F, 28 g KH

Roasted fennel

The preparation:
For 4 servings
Salt
Pepper
55g butter
600 g young fennel with green
2 eggs
165 g breadcrumbs
3 tablespoons freshly grated Parmesan
cheese

1. clean the fennel and remove the outer leaves Then quarter the tubers. Cut out the hard parts, cut off the fennel green and store.

2. bring salted water to the boil in a pot and cook the fennel for about 8 minutes. Afterwards take it out, quench and let it drain.

3.season the eggs with some salt and pepper and whisk them. Sprinkle breadcrumbs on a plate. In the meantime, heat butter in a pan.

4.turn the fennel pieces first in the egg mixture, then in the breadcrumbs and fry in the hot butter until the breadcrumbs are golden yellow. Remove from the pan, drain and sprinkle with parmesan.

5.chop the fennel greens and garnish the fried pieces with them. Goes well with meat or fish.

Preparation time
Approx. 20 minutes & cooking time + frying time
Per serving
Approx. 360 kcal/1470 kJ
14 g E, 19 g F, 35 g KH

Aubergines au gratin

The preparation
For 4 portions
800 g medium size
Aubergines
300 g mozzarella
1/2 bunch oregano
1/2 bunch basil
500 g tomatoes
100 g flour
100 ml olive oil
50 g grated Parmesan cheese
Salt

1. clean and wash the aubergines, dab dry well and cut lengthwise into thin slices. Put them in a key, sprinkle with salt and let them stand for about 15 minutes.

2. preheat the oven to 180 °C. Cut the mozzarella into small cubes. Wash and chop the herbs. Put the tomatoes in a bowl and puree them. Mix in the herbs.

3.Remove the aubergines from the bowl and dab dry. Turn aubergine slices in the flour. Heat the olive oil in a pan and fry the aubergines until golden brown. Then drain on kitchen paper.

4.grease the baking dish and first add aubergine slices, then tomato puree and finally mozzarella. Repeat the process until you can sprinkle the tomato puree with parmesan at the top. Bake in the oven for about 10 minutes.

Preparation time
Approx. 30 minutes & cooking time
Per serving
Approx. 445 kcal/1870 kJ
25 g E, 25 g F, 27 g KH

Gnocchi with gorganzola sauce

The preparation
For 4 portions
1 kg potatoes
250 g flour
Salt
Pepper
200 g Gorganzola
8 sage leaves
1 onion
1 garlic clove
1 tbsp olive oil
300 ml cream
100 ml dry white wine

1. wash the potatoes thoroughly and cook them with their skins for about 20 minutes until soft. Then drain, peel and mash with a potato masher. Let cool slightly, stir in the flour and salt the dough. Knead everything well. Form small oval dumplings from the dough and flatten with a fork. Let the gnocchi rest on a base for about 15 minutes.

2. cut the gorgonzola into small cubes. Peel and finely chop the onion and garlic. Wash the sage leaves and cut them into thin strips

3. heat the oil in a pot. Brown the onion and garlic in it. Add cream and wine and let it boil down slightly. Stir in sage, add gorgozola and let it melt while stirring. Add salt and pepper to taste.

4.cook the gnocchi in boiling salted water for about 5 minutes until they rise to the surface. Arrange them on plates with the sauce. Buon appetito :)

Preparation time
Approx. 30 minutes & cooking time
Per serving
Approximately 825 kcal/3465 kJ
23 g E, 43 g F, 90 g KH

Seafood salad Neapolitan style

For 4 portions
700 g mussels
350 g Vernus clams
350 g small squids
175 g raw shrimps
100ml dry white wine
Juice of 11/2 lemons
1 stick of celery
1/2 bunch flat parsley
salt, pepper
1 garlic clove
1 tsp mustard
3 tablespoons olive oil

1.brush the mussels thoroughly under water, do not use open mussels. Wash the squid and cut them into rings. Clean the shrimps.

2.in a large pot, boil 500 ml of water with wine, 1 tablespoon of lemon juice and a little salt. Simmer the squids covered in it for 2 minutes. Take them out with a skimmer and let them drain

3. leave the shrimps to soak in hot water for about 1 minute, then place them in a bowl with the squid. Boil the clams and mussels until all the mussels have risen. Drain the mussels. If there are still closed specimens, discard them. Remove the remaining mussels from their shells and add to the seafood.

3. peel and finely chop the garlic clove. Mix mustard with lemon juice, salt, pepper and oil well. Pour the garlic clove and marinade over the seafood, mix in and leave the salad to stand for at least 6 hours.

4.clean, wash and cut the celery into fine rings. Wash and finely chop the parsley. Add to the salad and serve.

Preparation time: approx. 45 minutes (plus cooking and marinating time)
Per portion approx. 450 kcal/1890 kJ
32 g E, 27 g F, 20 g KH

Insalata Caprese with buffalo mozzarella

For 4 portions
4 large tomatoes
300 g buffalo mozzarella
6 tbsp olive oil
salt, pepper
1 bunch of basil
Additional recommendation:
Olives or cucumber

1.wash and slice the tomatoes

2. drain the mozzarella and cut it into slices as well Wash the basil and pluck the leaves from the stalks. Arrange tomatoes and mozzarella alternately on a large plate and cover each mozzarella slice with a basil leaf (see picture above).

3.season the salad with salt and freshly ground pepper. Drizzle the olive oil over it.

Preparation time: approx. 20 minutes
Per portion approx. 370 kcal/1555 kJ
15 g E, 33 g F, 3 g KH

Potato salad Sicilian style

The preparation
For 4 portions
750 g potatoes
100 g pickled capers
150 g cherry tomatoes
10 black olives
2 tablespoons wine vinegar
3 tablespoons olive oil
4 pickled anchovies
1 red onion
Fresh marjoram
salt, pepper

1. wash the potatoes and cook them with their skins in boiling water for about 25 minutes Then drain and allow to cool. Then peel and cut into cubes.

2.put the potatoes with the drained capers in a bowl. Wash and halve the cherry tomatoes. Stone the olives, drain and chop the anchovies. Peel the onion and cut into rings.

3.add all the ingredients to the potatoes and capers and mix well. Add vinegar, oil, salt and pepper to taste. Leave Cira to stand for 1/2 hour. Garnish with marjoram and serve.

Preparation time
Approx. 20 minutes & cooking time + infusion time
Per serving
Approx. 625 kcal/2625 kJ
8 g E, 45 g F, 45 g KH

Tomato salad with arugula

The preparation
For 4 portions
500 g ripe tomatoes
2 bunches of rocket salad
3 tablespoons balsamic vinegar
6 tbsp olive oil
50 g Parmesan cheese
Salt
Pepper
1 onion

1.wash and slice the tomatoes Wash the arugula and cut into strips.

2. peel and finely chop the onion. Arrange tomatoes, rocket and onions on plates.

3.stir a marinade of balsamic vinegar, olive oil, salt and pepper and pour over the salad. Add parmesan cheese to taste.

Preparation time
Approx. 20 minutes
Per serving
Approx. 180 kcal/750 kJ
7 g E, 16 g F, 5 g KH

Pasta, risotto & Co.

Risotto nero with squid

750 g ready to cook
Cuttlefish with ink bags
2 cloves of garlic
1 onion
150 ml dry white wine
6 tbsp olive oil
Juice of 1 lime
750 ml fish stock
350 g risotto rice
Salt. Pepper

1. wash the squids and carefully place the ink bags in a bowl

2. cut the squid into strips. Peel and finely chop the garlic and onion.

3.mix the garlic with 3 tbsp. olive oil and the lime juice and pour over the squid strips Leave to soak for 1/2 hour.

4.heat the remaining olive oil in a pot and fry the onion in it. Put the squid strips into the pot and braise them. Pour in the wine and marinade. Now open the ink bag and add the ink. Pour in 150 ml fish stock, bring to the boil and let everything simmer for about 15 minutes.

5.put the rice into the pot and mix well. Gradually pour in the fish stock and let the rice absorb the liquid. After about 25 minutes the rice should be nice and creamy and the fish stock should be used up.

6.season the risotto with salt and pepper.

Preparation time: about 30 minutes
(plus marinating and cooking time)
Per portion approx. 540 kcal/2260 kJ
37 g E, 10 g F, 37 g KH

Risotto with truffle

3 tablespoons olive oil
350 g risotto rice
Salt
Pepper
300 ml cream
1-2 white or black truffles
1 l chicken broth
4 tablespoons freshly grated Parmesan cheese

1. heat the oil in a large pot and add the rice Stir-fry for a few minutes until the rice is nicely covered with fat. Stir in the cream and season with salt and pepper.
Clean the

2.truffles, slice a few thin slices and put them aside. Chop the rest and mix into the rice.

3.heat the chicken stock and add it slowly to the rice. After about 25 minutes the rice should be nice and creamy, but still al dente.

4.serve the risotto sprinkled with truffle slices and parmesan.

Preparation time: about 20 minutes
(plus cooking time)
Per portion approx. 425 kcal/1777 kJ
14 g E, 10 g F, 70 g KH

Penne with spicy sauce

500 g tomatoes
500 g penne
100 g streaky bacon
1 onion
1 garlic clove
1/2 bunch flat parsley
2 dried chillies
50 g freshly grated pecorino
2 tablespoons olive oil
salt, pepper

1.briefly dip the tomatoes in hot water, skin and seed them. Dice and puree the tomato pulp. Cut the bacon into cubes as well. Peel and finely chop the onion and garlic.

2.heat olive oil in a pan and fry the bacon in it. Add onions and garlic and let it braise for a few minutes.

3.stir in tomato puree, add chillies, salt and pepper.

4.simmer the mixture at low temperature for about 10 minutes.

5.cook penne in boiling salted water al dente

6.mix penne and chopped parsley into the sauce and sprinkle with cheese.

Preparation time: about 25 minutes
(plus braising and cooking time)
Per portion approx. 575 kcal/2405 kJ
24 g E, 13 g F, 90 g KH

spaghetti carbonara

50 g bacon
100 g cooked ham
400 g spaghetti
100 ml cream
1 garlic clove
2 tablespoons butter
3 eggs
40 g Parmesan cheese
40 g pecorino
salt, pepper

1.cut the bacon and ham into small cubes. Peel and finely chop the garlic. Heat butter in a pan and braise bacon and garlic in it.

2.In the meantime cook the spaghetti in boiling salted water until al dente. Add the noodles to the bacon in the pan and mix everything well.

3.whisk eggs, cream and half of the two cheeses together and season with salt and pepper. Add the cooked ham. Add this mixture to the spaghetti and mix everything well until the eggs begin to set.

4.fold the remaining cheese into the spaghetti and serve immediately.

Preparation time: about 20 minutes
(plus cooking time)
Per portion approx. 700 kcal/2950 kJ
31 g E, 33 g F, 70 g KH

spaghetti bolognese

1 onion
1 garlic clove
1 carrot
50 g bacon, 100 g chicken liver
2 tablespoons olive oil
250 g mixed minced meat
125 ml dry white wine
125 ml meat stock
400 g tomatoes
1/4 Tl dried oregano
1/4 tsp dried thyme
400 g spaghetti
50 g freshly grated Parmesan cheese
salt, pepper

1.peel and finely chop the onion and garlic. Peel the carrot and dice it like the bacon. Chop the liver finely.

2. heat olive oil in a pan. Fry the onion, garlic and bacon. Add the minced meat and liver and braise for 5-6 minutes.

3.pour the wine and broth into the pan and let it boil down a little. Drain the tomatoes in a sieve.

4.add the tomatoes to the meat and mix well. Season with salt, pepper and the dried herbs and let everything simmer at medium temperature for about 45 minutes.

5.in the meantime cook the spaghetti in plenty of boiling salted water until al dente. Arrange the pasta with the meat sauce on plates and sprinkle with parmesan.

Preparation time: about 20 minutes
(plus braising and cooking time)
Per portion approx. 850 kcal/3560 kJ
15 g E, 40 g F, 80 g KH

Tagliatelle with saffron sauce

For 4 portions
2 shallots
1 Msp. saffron threads
1 garlic clove
2 tablespoons olive oil
200 ml dry white wine
400 g tagliatelle
250 g mascarpone
50 g freshly grated Parmesan cheese
1 tablespoon freshly chopped flat parsley
2 tablespoons freshly chopped basil
salt, pepper

1.peel and finely chop the shallots and garlic. Heat the olive oil in a pan and sauté the shallots with the garlic for about 3 minutes. Add the saffron and wine. Season with salt and whistler. Bring the sauce to the boil until it is half boiled down.

2.Meanwhile, cook the tagliatelle in boiling salted water until al dente.

3.stir mascarpone into the sauce, bring to the boil and simmer for about 5 minutes.

4.mix the tagliatelle with the sauce in the pot, place on plates and arrange with the herbs Do not forget to add parmesan cheese!

Preparation time: about 20 minutes
(plus steaming and cooking time)
Per portion approx. 615 kcal/2583 kJ
35 g E, 40 g F, 25 g KH

rigatoni al pesto

50 g freshly grated Parmesan cheese
400 g Rigatoni
3 tbsp pine nuts
3 cloves of garlic
1 large bunch of basil
100 millilitres of olive oil
Salt

1.roast pine nuts in a pan without fat. Then chop finely with the garlic cloves. Wash and chop the basil.

2.mix pine nuts, garlic, basil and parmesan and slowly add the olive oil. Mix everything smooth and add salt.

3. cook the pasta in boiling salted water al dente.

4.place the pasta in a pan and mix well with the pesto over a low heat. Arrange on plates and serve.

Preparation time: about 20 minutes
(plus cooking time)
Per portion approx. 475 kcal/2000 kJ
12 g E, 29 g F, 45 g KH

Ravioli with spinach and sage butter

For 4 portions
400 g flour
4 eggs
1 Tl salt, El olive oil
1 onion, 1 garlic clove
1 tablespoon fresh rosemary needles
2 tablespoons olive oil
300 g minced beef
1 bay leaf
1/2 tl marjoram
1/2 tl of oregano
100 ml dry white wine
500 g spinach, 4 eggs, 50 g
breadcrumbs
2 tablespoons freshly grated Parmesan cheese
salt, pepper, nutmeg, 100 g butter
2 tablespoons fresh sage leaves

1. prepare a pasta dough from the ingredients of the dough Then let the dough rest.
2. clean and chop the onion, garlic and rosemary Heat oil in a pan and fry onion, garlic and rosemary. Then add minced meat and let it braise for 5 minutes. Add remaining herbs and wine and let the mixture simmer for about 10 minutes.
3.wash the spinach and cook in a pot at medium temperature. Then squeeze out well, chop and add to the minced meat. Puree the mixture and mix with eggs, breadcrumbs and parmesan. Season to taste with salt, pepper and nutmeg.
4. roll out the dough on a floured work surface into two thin sheets of dough. Place small piles of the filling on one pastry sheet at a distance of 3 cm and place the second pastry sheet on top. Press the edges firmly. Now cut the pastry sheet between the filling into wide strips. Cut out ravioli with a pastry wheel.
5. let the ravioli stand in boiling salted water for about 4 minutes. Heat butter in a pan and add sage leaves in fine strips. Present the ravioli with the sage butter and sprinkled with parmesan. Buon appetito.

Preparation time: about 40 minutes (plus cooking time)
Per portion approx. 870 kcal/3645 kJ
45 g E, 37 g F, 85 g KH

Cannelloni with tomato & mozzarella filling

For 4 portions
150 g flour
150 g durum wheat semolina
1 Tl salt
1,5 kg tomatoes
1 B2 Garlic cloves
2 tablespoons olive oil
salt, pepper
and basil
50g pickled anchovies
2 tablespoons pickled capers
100 g freshly grated Parmesan cheese
300 g mozzarella

1. prepare a pasta dough from flour, semolina, salt and 150 ml of lukewarm water and leave to rest

2.dip tomatoes in hot water, skin them and cut them into small pieces. Peel and chop garlic. Heat the oil in a pan and sauté the tomatoes with the garlic in it. Simmer at low temperature for about 25 minutes until a sauce forms. Season with salt and pepper to taste. Set some of the sauce aside.

3. cut basil, anchovies, capers and mozzarella into small pieces. Mix everything with the tomato sauce and let it cool down.

4. preheat the oven to 200° (fan oven 180°) Knead the pasta dough well and roll out on a floured work surface. Cut into squares of about 10 by 10 cm and cook them in boiling salted water for about 30 seconds.

5.grease an ovenproof dish. Lay out the pastry pieces, spread with the filling, roll up and place in the baking dish. Pour the rest of the tomato sauce over the cannelloni and sprinkle the grated cheese on top. Bake in the oven for about 30 minutes until golden brown.

Preparation time: about 30 minutes
(plus cooking and baking time)
Per portion approx. 800 kcal/3370 kJ
39 g E, 37 g F, 80 g KH

Pizza & Baked Goods

capricciosa pizza

For 1 round pizza dish
Yeast dough
250 g flour , 25 g yeast
4 tablespoons olive oil
Tomato sauce
400 g tomatoes (tin)
2 tablespoons olive oil
salt, pepper, 1/2 tsp. sugar
1 tsp dried thyme
1/2 tsp dried oregano, 2 cloves of garlic
Coating
10 artichoke hearts
100 g black olives without stone
150 g mozzarella
150 g cooked ham 6 anchovy fillets

1. sieve the flour into a bowl and make a depression in the middle Mix the yeast in about 1/8 l l lukewarm water and pour this pulp into the hollow. Sprinkle some flour over it and leave to rise in a warm place for 15 minutes. Then add 100 ml water, 1 pinch of salt and the oil to the pre-dough and work everything into a smooth dough. Knead the dough well for at least 10 minutes until it is firm but smooth. Cover the dough and leave it to rise in a warm place for at least 1 hour.

2.put the tomatoes in a pot with 1 tablespoon of olive oil and cook at high temperature for about 7 minutes. Season with salt, pepper, sugar and the herbs. Chop the garlic and add it to the tomato sauce.

Preheat the oven to 250 °C [fan oven 225 °C]. Grease a pizza dish with the remaining oil. Roll out the dough and place it in the form.

4. cut the ham into strips. Cut anchovy fillets, artichoke hearts and olives in half. Dice the mozzarella.

5.spread tomato sauce on the dough. Then spread the topping on the dough. Season with salt and pepper. Sprinkle the mozzarella on the end. Bake the pizza in the oven for about 25-35 minutes.

Preparation time: about 50 minutes
plus rest and baking time
Per portion approx. 600 kcal/2530 kJ
35gE, 30 g F.53 g KH

Pizza with mussels

For 1 round pizza dish
Yeast dough (see Pizza Capricciosa)
Tomato sauce [see Pizza Capricciosa]

500 g clams
100 g mozzarella
1 garlic clove
1/2 bunch flat parsley
1 tsp dried oregano
4 tablespoons olive oil
Pepper

1.prepare the yeast dough and tomato sauce according to the recipe of the Pizza Capricciosa (see above) Leave the yeast dough to rest for at least one hour.

2.clean the mussels and throw away any that are already open. Coarsely chop the garlic clove. Steam the mussels with oil, garlic and half of the parsley in a saucepan for about 5 minutes until all the mussels are open. If there are still closed mussels, please remove them.

3.roll out the dough and put it into the pizza form. Preheat oven to 250 °C [fan oven 225 °C].

4. remove the mussel meat from the shells with a knife. Dice mozzarella. Spread the tomato sauce on the dough and then spread the mussels on top. With salt. Season with pepper and oregano. Add some chopped parsley and mozzarella. Bake in the oven for about 20 minutes.

Preparation time: about 50 minutes
(plus rest, cooking and baking time)
Per portion approx. 475 kcal/2000 kJ
27 g E,17 g F.55 g KH

Pizza Calzone with meat filling

For 1 calzone
1 yeast dough
50 g grated pecorino
100 g rocket salad
150 g cooked ham
1 egg
1 tbsp. tomato paste
1 garlic clove
1 tsp thyme
1 T1 oregano
1 tbsp olive oil
2 tomatoes
2 spring onions
Salt
Pepper

1.Prepare the 1st yeast dough (as described on the page Pizza Capricciosa) and let the dough rest for about 1 hour.

2. cut the ham into small cubes. Clean the spring onions and cut them into rings. Finely chop the garlic. Simmer the tomatoes, skin them and cut them into cubes. Wash and chop the arugula.

3.Roll out the dough on a floured work surface to a circle of about 35 cm diameter. Beat the egg and coat the edges of the dough with it. Spread tomato paste on the dough. Preheat the oven to 250 °C [fan oven 225 °C].

4.cover one half of the dough with the ingredients. Add salt, pepper, herbs and cheese as desired. Fold the dough in half and press the edges firmly together. Brush the calzone with the remaining egg.

5. grease a baking tray with oil and place the calzone on top. bake in the oven for about 30 minutes. Buon appetito!

Preparation time: about 30 minutes
plus rest and baking time
Per portion approx. 320 kcal/1340 kJ
26 g E.19 g F,14 g KH

focaccia alla romana

For 1 plate (15 pieces)
550 g red and white onions
450 g durum wheat flour
150 g freshly grated
Parmesan cheese
25 g yeast
2 tablespoons olive oil
3 El rosemary needles
4 cloves of garlic
1/2 bunch flat parsley
Salt

1.form a yeast dough (as described on the page Pizza Capricciosa) from flour, yeast, 300 ml of lukewarm water, salt and half the rosemary needles and leave to rise in a warm place.

2. cut the onions into thin rings for the topping. Heat the oil in a pan and fry the onions in it. Add the garlic and let it braise for another 5 minutes with the lid closed.

3. preheat the oven to 200 °C [fan oven 180 °C]. Roll out the dough on a floured work surface to a thickness of about 0.5 cm and place on a greased baking tray. Spread the steamed onions over the dough.

4.spread the chopped parsley with the remaining rosemary and cheese on the onions. bake in the oven for about 30 minutes. Then cut into squares and serve.

Preparation time: about 40 minutes
plus resting-' braising time
Per piece approx. 180 kcal/750 kJ
8 g E.6 g F,25 g KH

Calabrese

For 1 round pizza dish
1 yeast dough
Tomato sauce
1 onion
1 garlic clove 150 g tuna
(canned)
4 anchovy fillets
1 tbsp. capers
1 tablespoon dried thyme
50 g freshly grated Parmesan cheese
50 g black olives without stone
salt, pepper

1.prepare the yeast dough and tomato sauce (as described on the page Pizza Capricciosa) Let the dough rise for at least 1 hour.

2. chop the onion, garlic and anchovy fillets. Drain the tuna and capers. Preheat the oven to 250 °C [fan oven 225 °C].

Roll out the dough and place in the greased tin. Spread the tomato sauce on top.

Spread the remaining ingredients on the dough and season with salt, pepper and thyme to taste. Sprinkle the cheese on top and bake the pizza in the oven for about 25 minutes.

Preparation time: about 50 minutes
plus rest and baking time
Per portion approx. 505 kcal/2112 kJ
23 g E 25 g F, 50 g KH

Pizza frutti di mare

For a round pizza dish
Yeast dough
Tomato sauce
100 g small calamari ready to cook
(Squids)
100 g clams from the glass
200 g fresh shrimps
1 bunch of basil
1 tbsp olive oil
3 tablespoons freshly grated pecorino
salt, pepper

1.prepare the yeast dough and tomato sauce (as described on the page Pizza Capricciosa) and then let the dough rest for at least an hour

2. wash the cuttlefish and steam in a little water for about 5 minutes, peel the gamels and remove the intestines. Clean the mussels thoroughly.

3. preheat oven to 200 °C [fan oven 180 °C]. Roll out the dough and place it in the greased tin. Then spread the tomato sauce on top and cover with seafood.

4.season to taste with basil, salt and pepper. Spread olive oil and cheese on top and bake in the oven for about 30 minutes.

Preparation time: about 30 minutes
plus resting' steaming and baking time
Per portion approx. 415 kcal/1745 kJ
27 g E, 13 g F, 50 g KH

Fleisch und Geflügel

Chicken pan piquant and spicy

For 4 portions

1 ready-to-cook chicken
(about 1.2 kg)
300 g tomatoes
150 ml dry white wine
50 g provolone
1 dried pepper
1 tablespoon freshly chopped parsley
1 tablespoon freshly chopped lovage
1 tablespoon freshly chopped basil
salt, pepper
1 onion
5 tablespoons olive oil

1.salt and pepper the chicken and cut it into 8 parts. Simmer the tomatoes, peel, remove seeds and cut into eighths. Peel onion and cut into rings.

2.heat oil in a pan and fry the chicken parts in it. Add onion rings and let them braise. Add wine and small crumbled peppers.

3.bring the mixture to the boil until the wine is almost cooked. Then add tomatoes and herbs.

4. braise the chicken covered for about 1 hour at medium temperature. After about 40 minutes cooking time, dice the provolone cheese and stir in. Season the chicken pan at the end of the cooking time to taste. Enjoy!

Preparation time approx. 30 minutes
Plus cooking time
Per portion approx. 430 kcal/1790 kJ
21 g E, 21 g F, 6 g KH

Roast pork in milk

For 4 portions
1 kg leg of pork without
Bones
1 garlic clove
Flour for dusting
750 ml milk
500 ml dry white wine
5 tablespoons butter
1 sprig of rosemary
salt, pepper

1. place the meat in a large bowl and add chopped garlic Pour wine over it and let the meat marinate in the fridge for about 48 hours.

2. remove the meat from the marinade and dust the flour over it. Heat the butter in a large roasting pan and fry the meat well on all sides.

3. clean the rosemary and add it to the meat with the milk. Season to taste with salt and pepper. Cover the roaster and cook the pork in the oven at 170 °C for about 2 hours.

4. take the meat out of the roaster and put it on a plate. Let the gravy boil down. Cut the meat into slices and serve with the milk sauce.

Preparation time: about 20 minutes
plus marinating and cooking time
Per portion approx. 510 kcal/2140 kJ
48 g E, 30 g F,12 g KH

Rabbit with tomatoes and herbs

For 4 portions
1 ready-to-cook rabbit
1 sprig of rosemary
2 cloves of garlic
2 Thyme wels
2 bay leaves
200 ml dry rosé wine
300 g tomatoes
1 onion
1 carrot
2 sticks of celery
3 tablespoons olive oil
2 tablespoons grappa
salt, pepper

1. cut the rabbit into 8 pieces and rub with salt and pepper. Peel and chop the garlic.

2.clean the herbs and chop them coarsely.

3.blanch tomatoes hot, peel, seed and chop. Peel onion, wash and chop carrot and celery.

4.heat the oil in a roasting pan and fry the rabbit parts well. Then remove from the roaster. Add the garlic, herbs, onion and vegetables and braise for 3 minutes. Then add wine and grappa. Add the tomatoes and mix well.

5. put the meat back into the roaster and season with salt and pepper to taste Let the rabbit stew covered for about 45 minutes.

Preparation time: about 30 minutes
plus cooking time
Per portion approx. 735 kcal/3088 kJ
80 g E, 42 g F, 7 g KH

Schnitzel with Marsala sauce

For 4 portions
3 tablespoons clarified butter
4 pork escalope
4 tablespoons flour
50 ml meat stock
75 ml Marsala
Salt
Pepper

1. beat the escalope flat, rub with salt and pepper and turn in the flour.

2. heat clarified butter in a frying pan and fry the escalopes on both sides for about 4 minutes. Remove from the pan and keep warm.

3.deglaze the gravy with Marsala and stock and let it boil down by a third. Arrange the escalopes and serve with the marsala sauce.

Preparation time: approx. 10 minutes
plus frying time
Per portion approx. 570 kcal/2400 kJ
40 g E, 33 g F'28 g KH

Roast beef in Barolo

For 4 portions
50 g bacon, 2 carrots
1/2 stick of celery
1 kg shoulder of beef
1 tsp peppercorns
2 bay leaves
1 sprig of rosemary
1 thyme branch, 750 ml Barolo
4 tablespoons olive oil, 2 tablespoons clarified butter
2 tablespoons cognac, 2 stems parsley
10 juniper berries
1 cinnamon stick, 2 cloves, 1 pinch
Sugar
2 cloves of garlic
3 El Marsala, salt, pepper
Flour for dusting

1. cut garlic cloves in half, cut bacon into strips, peel carrots and clean celery. Wash and chop the vegetables. Prick the meat with a knife and lard with garlic and bacon strips.

2.put the meat in a bowl, add the vegetables. Crush peppercorns and juniper berries and add them to the meat with bay leaves, cinnamon, cloves, sugar and herb twigs. Add wine and Marsala and marinate the meat covered for 12 hours in the refrigerator. It is also best to turn it once.

3. remove meat from marinade and rub with salt and pepper. Pour the marinade through a sieve. Collect the liquid. Drain the vegetables and herb twigs.
4.heat oil and clarified butter in a roasting pan and fry the vegetables with the herbs in it. Dust the meat with flour and fry it. Deglaze with cognac.

5.pour marinade to the meat and add parsley. Stew meat at medium temperature covered for about 2 hours 30 minutes. Remove roast and herb twigs from the pot and puree the sauce. Season to taste with salt and pepper. Cut the roast open and garnish with the sauce. Polenta goes perfectly with it.

Preparation time: approx. 30 minutes
plus marinating and braising time
Per portion approx. 1030 kcal/4335 kJ
57 g E,62 g F'21 g KH

Stuffed fillet of beef Lombard style

For 4 portions
1 bunch of parsley
1 tarragon branch
4 sage leaves
3 tablespoons freshly
grated pannesan
50 g breadcrumbs
75 g pecorino
1 kg fillet of beef
150 g raw ham
2 branches of oregano
100 ml dry red wine
salt, pepper
3 tablespoons olive oil

1. wash the herbs, chop them finely and mix with parmesan and breadcrumbs. Then season with salt and pepper.

2.cut the pecorino into strips. Cut the meat lengthwise at the top and add the parmesan herb filling and the pecorino strips. Cut the ham into slices and wrap them around the meat. Tie it with kitchen string.

3. preheat the oven to 180 °C [fan oven 160 °C]. Heat the oil in a frying pan and fry the remaining sage leaves and oregano twigs in it. Then brown the meat. Roast the roast in the oven for about 35 minutes. Then remove the meat from the roaster and let it rest for 10 minutes.

4.boil the meat stock with wine and a little water and pass it through a sieve. Bring the sauce to the boil in a pot and let it boil down a little. Cut the meat into slices and serve with the sauce. Buon appetito.

Preparation time:

about 20 minutes

plus cooking time

Per portion approx. 925 kcal/3885 kJ

100 g E, 49 g F,15 g KH

Stuffed veal breast Ligurian style

For 4 portions
1 garlic clove
750 g breast of veal with
bag to fill
100 g pork tenderloin
100 g sweetbread
100 g calf's brain
75 g peas
15 g dried porcini
30 g butter
200 ml dry white wine
1 tablespoon freshly chopped marjoram
2 tablespoons chopped pistachios
2 l vegetable broth
3 tablespoons freshly grated Parmesan cheese
3 eggs
salt, pepper, nutmeg

1.soak the calf's brain and sweetbreads in water for about 2 hours, drain and clean. Rub veal breast with garlic clove. Dice the fillet and soak the dried mushrooms in hot water.
2.heat butter in a pan and fry the fillet cubes in it. Add the veal brain and sweetbreads and braise. Pour the wine. Add the finely chopped mushrooms. Simmer for 2 minutes. Then puree the pan mixture.
3.mix the meat puree in a bowl with peas, marjoram, pistachios, parmesan and eggs and work into a smooth dough. Pour the filling into the veal breast and seal it with kitchen string.
4.place the breast of veal in a large pot and cover with the stock. Close the pot and simmer the veal breast in it for about 1 minute. Then remove the lid and simmer the meat for another hour. During this time, prick the meat more often.
5. take the breast of veal out of the pot and let it cool down. Then cut into slices and serve.

Preparation time: approx. 35 minutes
plus soaking and cooking time
Per portion approx. 1
442 kcal/1843 kJ
49 g E,25 g F'4 g KH

Lamb stew with mushrooms

For 4 portions
1 kg leg of lamb without
Bones
125 ml dry white wine
200 g onions
500 g small mushrooms
salt, pepper
1 tablespoon freshly
chopped rosemary
2 El Marsala
3 tablespoons olive oil

1.dice the leg of lamb, clean the mushrooms, peel and chop the onions.

2.preheat the oven to 190 °C convection oven 170 °C Heat olive oil in a pot and fry the meat well. Add onions and braise while turning. Add mushrooms and wine and fill up with enough water to cover the meat well. Season with salt, pepper and rosemary to taste.

3.cover the pot and cook the ragout in the oven for about 1 hour until the meat is nice and soft. Then season to taste with the Marsala.

Preparation time: about 25 minutes
plus braising and cooking time
Per portion approx. 450 kcal/1900 kJ
57 g E,13 g F,5 g KH

Fish and seafood

Sole fillets au gratin

For 4 portions
8 sole fillets without skin
1 garlic clove
4 tablespoons freshly chopped flat
parsley
4 tablespoons freshly chopped dill
6 tablespoons grated pecorino
6 tbsp olive oil
8 tablespoons breadcrumbs
Salt
Pepper

1. preheat the oven to 240 °C (fan oven 220 °C). Season fish fillets with salt and pepper and place on an oiled baking tray.

Peel and chop the garlic. Mix with breadcrumbs, herbs and pecorino and place on the fish fillets. Then add olive oil.

3.bake the sole fillets in the oven for about 15 minutes.

Preparation time: about 15 minutes
plus baking time
Per portion approx. 705 kcal/2960 kJ
65 g E' 30 g F' 41 g KH

Sea bass with olive sauce

For 1. portion 4 ready-to-cook sea bass
Worcester sauce
100 g cooked ham
100 g olives
150 g flour
200 ml dry white wine
200 ml vegetable broth
1 bunch of tarragon
1 bunch of spring onions
1 fresh pepper
1 tablespoon capers (from the glass)
2 tablespoons olive oil
2 tbsp. tomato paste
salt, pepper
Juice of 1 lemon

1. preheat the oven grill on the highest level. Season fish with salt and pepper and place in a bowl. Pour lemon juice and Worcester sauce over the fish and leave to stand for 20 minutes.

2.wash the tarragon and use one sprig per fish as filling. Take the fish out of the marinade and turn them in the flour. Grill under the hot grill in the oven for about 15 minutes.

3.chop the spring onions, dice the ham and chop the pepper finely. Stone and chop the olives. Drain the capers.

4.heat the oil in a pot and fry the spring onions in it. Add ham, pepper, olives and capers and braise briefly. Stir in tomato paste and add wine and stock. Season the sauce with salt and pepper to taste. Arrange the fish with the sauce on plates and serve.

Preparation time: approx. 30 minutes
plus grill and braising time
Per portion approx. 550 kcal/2310 kJ
50 g E,16 g F'43 g KH

Red mullets with pancetta

For 4 portions
4 red mullets ready to cook (a 300 g)
1 untreated lime
1 sprig of rosemary
2 cloves of garlic
1/2 bunch dill
50 g breadcrumbs
100 g pancetta
(bacon in thin slices)
salt, pepper

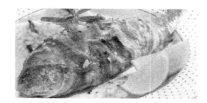

1.place the fish in a large mould and season with salt and pepper. Wash the lime hot, peel it and cut one part into thin strips, squeeze the other.

2.chop garlic cloves and rosemary finely. Mix garlic with lime pieces and juice and the rosemary. Pour the whole over the fish and leave it in the fridge for about one hour.

3.chop the dill and mix with the breadcrumbs. Preheat oven to 180 °C [fan oven 160 °C]. Take the fish out of the marinade and turn in the breadcrumbs.

Wrap the pancetta slices around the fish and place the fish in the fat pan of the oven.

5.pour the marinade over the fish and bake in the oven for about 20 minutes

Preparation time: about 20 minutes
plus marinating and baking time
Per portion approx. 460 kcal/1920 kJ
62 g E, 19 g F, 11 g KH

Grilled tuna with anchovies

For 4 portions
4 slices of tuna fish
(a 150 g)
200 ml dry white wine
1 sprig of rosemary
1 garlic clove
4 tablespoons olive oil
3 anchovies without bones
Juice of 2 limes
salt, pepper

1. wash tuna and preheat the oven grill on the highest level.

2. chop rosemary and garlic finely.

3.mix a marinade of wine, lime juice, rosemary and garlic and season with salt and pepper. Place tuna slices in this marinade and leave to marinate for 3 hours. Then take the fish out and grill under the grill for about 10 minutes on each side. Finally, pour the marinade over the fish.

4.heat olive oil in a pan and braise the anchovies in it for 3 minutes on both sides. Then mash them with a fork. Spread the tuna with the anchovy paste and serve.

Preparation time: about 20 minutes
plus marinating time
Per portion approx. 600 kcal/2510 kJ
56 g E,38 g F,2 g KH

Stuffed trout with crayfish tails

4 large kitchenettes
Trout without bones
4 crayfish tails
1 egg
1/2 bunch parsley
1/2 bunch tarragon
3 El Grappa
Worcester sauce
Juice of 1 lime
50 ml dry white wine
2 tablespoons of olive oil
40 g butter
80 g freshly grated provolone
150 g cream
1 tablespoon flour
1 ElTomato paste
salt, pepper

1.Washing fish. Remove the meat from the shells of the crayfish tails. Chop the herbs finely and preheat the oven to 200 °C [fan oven 180 °C].

2.mix the cheese with the herbs, 1 tablespoon grappa, the egg, a few drops of Worcester sauce, salt and pepper in a bowl and fill the trout with it. Put one crayfish tail into each trout and place them in a suitable dish.

3.season the fish with salt, pepper and lime juice. Pour wine, remaining grappa and olive oil over it and cover everything with foil. Roast in the oven for about 25 minutes. Afterwards keep warm on a plate.

4. drain the roast stock through a sieve. Mix the cream with the flour and bring to the boil in a saucepan. Season the stock with Worcester sauce and tomato paste and stir in the butter.

5.fold in the cream and serve the sauce with the stuffed trout.

Preparation time: approx. 30 minutes

plus frying and cooking time

Per portion approx. 620 kcal/2607 kJ

61 g E, 33 g F'15 g KH

Swordfish in Marsala

For 4 portions
4 swordfish steaks
(a175g)
2 anchovies (from the glass)
3 tablespoons lemon juice
1/2 bunch parsley
1 onion
1 garlic clove
4 tablespoons olive oil
125 ml dry white wine
75 ml Marsala
salt, pepper

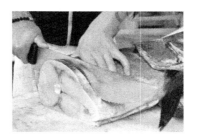

1.sprinkle swordfish with lemon juice. Chop parsley, onions finely. Rub the fish slices with salt and pepper.

2.heat the oil in a pan and fry the fish steaks for 2 minutes on each side. Add the onion and garlic and fry. Then add wine and Marsala and simmer everything covered for 5 minutes.

3.drain the anchovies and then mash them. Then remove the fish from the sauce and keep warm. Stir parsley and anchovies into the sauce and bring to the boil.

4. reduce the sauce by a third while stirring Finally serve with the swordfish steaks. Buon appetito!

Preparation time: approx. 20 minutes
plus cooking time
Per portion approx. 355 kcal/1484 kJ
36 g E, 21 g F, 3 g KH

Fried prawns Venetian style

For 4 portions
24 raw prawns with shell
2 lemons
2 dill branches
3 tablespoons flour
3 eggs
salt, pepper
Frying oil

1. wash the shrimps and remove the heads, shells and intestines Then dust with flour.

2. whisk eggs and season with salt and pepper. Heat the oil in a large pot.

3.turn the scampi in the egg mixture, drain briefly and fry in the hot oil for about 3 minutes until golden brown. Then drain on kitchen paper.

4.serve prawns with lemon halves and chopped dill. Perfect with fresh ciabatta.

Preparation time: about 20 minutes
plus frying time
Per portion approx. 775 kcal/3258 kJ
130 g E,18 g F,22 g KH

Stuffed mussels with tomatoes

For 4 portions
1.5 kg mussels
5 eggs
125 g freshly grated
Pecorino
250 g breadcrumbs
400 g of strained tomatoes
3 tablespoons freshly chopped
Parsley
1 garlic clove
3 tablespoons olive oil
1 tablespoon freshly chopped oregano
salt, pepper

1.brush the mussels well under running water. Remove opened mussels. Preheat oven to 200 °C [fan oven 180 °C]. Bring water to the boil in a large saucepan and cook the mussels for about 5 minutes until they have opened. Discard unopened mussels.

Whisk the eggs and mix with the breadcrumbs and cheese. Add parsley and beat everything to a creamy mixture. Place the opened mussels on a baking tray and spread the egg mixture over them. Close the mussel shells slowly and bake in the oven for about 15 minutes.

3.heat oil in a saucepan and fry the finely chopped garlic in it. Add the tomatoes and simmer for about 10 minutes at medium temperature. Season to taste with salt, pepper and oregano.

Preparation time: about 30 minutes
plus baking and cooking time
Per portion approx. 770 kcal/3225 kJ
60 g E, 31 g F, 65 g KH

Stuffed squid with potatoes

For 4 portions
2 rolls from the previous day
3 cloves of garlic
1 bunch of flat parsley
1 onion
2 eggs
2 large tomatoes
12 medium size ready-to-cook
Cuttlefish with tentacles
500 g potatoes
1 dried pepper
4 tablespoons olive oil
salt, pepper

1.soak the rolls for the filling in warm water. Chop garlic and parsley finely. After about 10 minutes, squeeze the bread rolls well. Then mix with the eggs, a third of the garlic and half of the parsley in a bowl, season with salt and pepper to taste.

2.wash the squid well and fill with the mixture. Make sure that only half of the body is filled, as the filling expands during baking. Plug the openings with wooden skewers. Preheat the oven to 160 °C [fan oven 140 °C].

3. peel onion and cut into rings. Simmer the tomatoes, remove skin and seeds and dice the flesh. Wash and peel the potatoes and cut them into slices about 1 cm thick. Crumble the pepper.

4. put onion rings, diced tomatoes and garlic in a large dish. Sprinkle with salt and pepper and add 3 tablespoons of water. Layer the potato slices and place the squids on top. Sprinkle with pepper and drizzle with olive oil.

5. cover the mould with foil and cook the cuttlefish in the oven for about 1 hour Serve hot, sprinkled with the remaining parsley.

Preparation time: about 35 minutes
plus soaking and baking time
Per portion approx . 805 kcal/3383 kJ
104 g E,22 g F, 47 g KH

Gilthead seabream with onions

For 4 portions
1 onion
1 garlic clove
1 sprig of rosemary
1 thyme branch
1 fresh pepper
1 ready-to-cook gilthead seabream
(approx. 600 g)
1 vegetable onion
1 large potato
1/2 stick of celery
1 l vegetable broth
5 tablespoons olive oil
pepper, salt

1. chop onion, garlic and herbs for the filling. Then mix them together and add 3 tbsp. olive oil. Clean, wash, seed and finely chop the pepper. Add to the mixture.

Preheat 2nd oven to 180 °C [fan oven 160 °C]. Salt the fish well from the inside and add as much filling as possible. Cut the vegetable onion into rings. Heat 2 tbsp. oil in a roasting pan and braise the onion rings with the remaining filling in it. Place the fish on top and pepper.

3.wash, peel and dice the potatoes. Clean, wash and chop the celery. Put potatoes and celery around the fish and cook the fish in the oven for about 25 minutes. Meanwhile, gradually pour on the vegetable stock. Serve the fish with vegetables and roast stock.

Preparation time: about 30 minutes
plus braising and frying time
Per portion approx. 345 kcal/1449 kJ
30 g E, 20 g F, 14 g KH

Dolci

Cream puffs to fill

For 6 portions of 200 ml milk
4 tablespoons butter
1 pinch of salt
140 g flour
1 tsp baking powder 4 eggs
grease for the mould

1. put milk and butter in a saucepan, add salt and bring to the boil

2. sieve flour with baking powder into a bowl. Add the flour mixture to the milk mixture while stirring and stir until the mixture comes off the bottom of the pot.

3. put this doughball in a bowl and let it cool down. Now gradually stir in the eggs. Preheat the oven to 225 °C [fan oven 200 °C]. Grease a baking tray.

4.use a spoon to cut off small piles of dough and place them on the baking tray. Bake the wound bags for about 25 minutes until golden brown. Then allow to cool, cut open and fill as required.

Preparation time: about 20 minutes
plus baking time
Per portion approx. 625 kcal/2625 kJ
13 g E, 50 g F, 31 g KH

Figs stuffed with chocolate

For 4 portions
8 fresh figs
2 tablespoons honey
2 tablespoons dry Marsala
35 g chopped walnuts
80 g Mascarpone
80 g whole milk chocolate

1.Wash figs. Then cut the bottom straight so that they can stand. In addition, cut crosswise at the top about 2 cm deep. Preheat oven to 200 °C [fan oven 180 °C].

2.Mix the chopped nuts, honey, Marsala and mascarpone well together. Fill the figs with this mixture. Then place on a baking tray and bake in the oven for about 12 minutes.

3.melt the chocolate in a bain-marie and spread it over the baked figs
give. Figs ready to eat immediately. Buon appetito!

Preparation time: approx. 30 minutes
plus baking time
Per portion approx. 415 kcal/1735 kJ
13 g E, 18 g F, 50 g KH

Tiramisù

For 4 portions
4 Egg yolk
100 g sponge fingers
100 g sugar
250 ml cold espresso
300 g mascarpone
2 tbsp. brandy
Cocoa powder for dusting

1. stir the egg yolks in a bowl until very frothy. Then gradually stir in the sugar. Place this cream in a water bath and continue stirring until the sugar has dissolved well. Add mascarpone by the spoonful to the cream and stir in with a hand mixer.

2.line a rectangular form with half of the sponge cake. Stir the brandy into the espresso and soak the biscuits with a good half of the liquid. Spread half of the mascarpone cream on top. Place the remaining biscuits on top and pour the remaining coffee over them. Spread the rest of the cream on top.

Put the tiramisù in the fridge for at least 8 hours. Sift the cocoa powder over it and serve at room temperature.

Preparation time: about 30 minutes
plus cooling time
Per portion approx. 685 kcal/2879 kJ
32 g E, 37 g F, 44 g KH

Panforte Tuscan fruit cake

For 1 springform pan
28 cm diameter (12 pieces)
100 g cocoa powder
100 g hazelnuts
100 g pine nuts
150 g walnuts
150 g dried figs
150 g honey
150 g icing sugar
250 g almonds
300 g mixed candied fruits
1 pinch of white pepper
1 pinch ground nutmeg
1 wafer (28 cm diameter)
Icing sugar for dusting

1.roast nuts, kernels and almonds in a large pan. Then let it cool down and chop finely.

2.cut the dried figs and the candied fruit into small cubes and place them in a bowl. Add nuts, almonds, seeds, cocoa and spices and mix everything. Preheat oven to 150 °C [fan oven 130 °C].

3.put honey and icing sugar in a pot and put it in a water bath. Stir until the honey is melted and has combined well with the icing sugar.

4.line the springform pan with a large wafer. Mix nut mixture and honey and icing sugar mixture together. Add 2 tablespoons of water and stir everything to a smooth mixture.

5.spread the mixture on the wafer and bake Panforte in the oven for about 30 minutes.

6.remove from the pan, let cool and dust with icing sugar.

Preparation time: about 30 minutes
plus baking time
Per piece approx. 525 kcal/2200 kJ
11 g E, 32 g F, 50 g KH

Panna Cotta with Marsala and mint

For 4 portions
250 g cream
250 ml milk
1 vanilla pod
1/2 tl grated rind
of 1 untreated lemon
2 El Marsala
3 tablespoons sugar
4 peppermint leaves
4 sheets of white gelatine

1. soak gelatine in cold water. Put cream and milk in a pot. Add pulp to the vanilla pod. Then stir in the sugar and lemon peel and bring the mixture to the boil. Simmer at low temperature for about 10 minutes.

2.squeeze the gelatine and stir it into the cream-milk mixture until it dissolves in it. Then remove the pot from the stove.

3. pour the panna cotta into cold rinsed round baking pans and place in the fridge for at least 6 hours. Finally, turn the panna cotta out onto plates. Garnish with Marsala and mint leaves.

Preparation time: approx. 30 minutes
plus cooking and cooling time
Per portion approx. 289 kcal/ 1210 kJ
5 g E, 22 g F, 22 g KH

Lemon cake light and fresh

For 1 box mould (8 pieces)
12 large eggs
1 sachet vanilla sugar
150 g chopped almonds
175 g sugar
300 g wheat flour
1/2 tl salt
grease for the mould
Icing sugar for dusting
grated rind and
Juice of 4 lemons
grated rind of
1 untreated orange

1. preheat the oven to 170 °C [fan oven 150 °C] and grease a box mould [approx. 25 cm long].

2. separate the eggs. Beat the egg yolks in a bowl until frothy. Gradually add sugar, vanilla sugar, almonds, lemon zest, juice and orange zest. Mix all this to a creamy mixture.

Sift the flour into a bowl and add the salt. Then add to the lemon mixture and mix well. Beat the egg whites until stiff and fold in until a smooth dough is obtained.

4. fill the dough into the tin and bake in the oven for about 50 minutes. Then take the cake out of the oven. Turn out immediately onto a cake rack and dust with icing sugar.

Preparation time: about 20 minutes
plus baking time
Per piece approx. 465 kcal/1955 kJ
19 g E, 22 g F, 50 g KH

Zabaione with Marsala and lemon

For 4 portions
100 ml Marsala
4 Egg yolk
40 g sugar
juice of 1/2 untreated lemon

1. beat the egg yolks and sugar in a metal bowl until foamy
Add 1 tbsp. warm water and place the bowl in a bain-marie.
Continue beating the egg-sugar mixture with a whisk.

2.gradually add the Marsala and stir the cream for about 10
minutes until it has approximately doubled in size. Season to
taste with lemon juice.

3. remove the bowl from the water bath. Pour the zabaglione
into glasses and serve warm immediately. Goes well with
sponge fingers or Amarettini.

Preparation time: about 20 minutes
Per portion approx. 118 kcal/497 kJ
4 g E, 7 g F, 11 g KH

Cantuccini Tuscan style

For 50 pieces
2 eggs
90 g sugar
125 g whole almonds
225 g wheat flour
Juice and grated rind
of 1/2 untreated orange
1/2 tl baking powder

1. preheat the oven to 175 °C [convection oven 155 °C]. Put eggs and sugar in a bowl and stir until frothy. Stir in orange juice and orange peel.

Sift the flour and baking powder into the egg cream and mix briefly. Then knead the dough with your hands further to a loose dough.

3.dip the almonds in hot water and then remove the shell. Mix the almonds into the dough. Form the dough into 3 rolls (about 4 cm diameter) and place them on a greased baking tray. Bake in the oven for about 30 minutes.

Take the 4. dough rolls out of the oven and let them cool down. Then cut into finger-thick slices. Put the cantuccini back on the baking tray and bake in the oven for another 10 minutes until crispy.

Preparation time: about 20 minutes
plus baking time
Per piece approx. 43 kcal/173 kJ
1 g E, 2 g F, 5 g KH

Melon sorbet Sicilian style

For 4 portions
(Water-. honey or
cantaloupe melon)
75 g sugar
75 g icing sugar
750 g melon meat
Juice of 1 lemon

1.mix sugar and icing sugar and heat with 150 ml water in a pot while stirring until the sugar dissolves Simmer the mixture for 3 minutes. Let it cool down afterwards.

2. remove skin and seeds from melons and cut them into small cubes. Then puree in a blender. Mix with the lemon juice. Add cold sugar syrup and stir well.

3. pour the mixture into a bowl and freeze it in the freezer. Then stir well and freeze again until the sorbet has set.

4. put the melon sorbet in the fridge for about 30 minutes before serving Arrange and serve well.

Preparation time: about 15 minutes
plus freezing time
Per portion approx. 185 kcal/770 kJ
1 g E, 1 g F, 44 g KH

Ricotta ice cream with espresso

For 4 portions
100 g sugar
125 ml espresso
500 g ricotta
1 Tl vanilla sugar
2 tablespoons cocoa powder
3 tablespoons cream
4 El Marsala
4 Egg yolk

1. allow the espresso to cool. Pass the ricotta through a sieve and mix it evenly with the espresso.

2. beat the sugar and egg yolks until foamy. Whip the cream until stiff, add vanilla sugar and Marsala. Mix the espresso ricotta and egg foam together and fold in the cream.

3. pour the mixture into a bowl or rectangular form and cover with cling film. Freeze in the freezer for about 3 hours.

4.then spread the ricotta ice cream with an ice cream scoop on small bowls and sprinkle with cocoa powder.

Preparation time: approx. 15 minutes
plus time to freeze
Per portion approx. 428 kcal/ 1798 kJ
20 g E, 25 g F' 33 g KH

Amaretto parfait with figs

For 4 portions
125 g sugar
300 g cream
pulp from 1/2 vanilla pod
2 tablespoons cognac
3 El Amaretto
3 eggs
4 figs

1.Separate an egg. Beat two eggs and the egg yolk with 90 g sugar in a metal bowl in a warm water bath until foamy. Add Amaretto slowly and stir the cream for another 5 minutes.

Mix 2.cream with vanilla pulp and stir with egg cream. Pour the mixture into 4 pudding moulds and freeze for about 3 hours.

3. wash and slice the figs. Marinate in a bowl with cognac and remaining sugar.

4 After the freezing time, briefly dip the pudding moulds in warm water and turn the parfait out onto plates. Serve with the marinated figs. Serve with any fruit sauce.

Preparation time: approx. 20 minutes
plus marinating and freezing time
Per portion approx. 425 kcal/1787 kJ
8 g E, 28 g F, 30 g KH

Imprint

Information according to § 5 TMG

Nonna Maria is represented by Carlo Sorce
Main road 133
76327 Pfinztal

Contact
E-mail: carlo-sorce@hotmail.com

Liability for contents

As a service provider, we are responsible for our own content on these pages according to § 7 para.1 TMG (German Telemedia Act) and general laws. According to §§ 8 to 10 TMG, we are not obliged to monitor transmitted or stored external information or to investigate circumstances that indicate illegal activity. Obligations to remove or block the use of information according to general laws remain unaffected. However, any liability in this respect is only valid from the time of the
Knowledge of a concrete violation of the law is possible. If we become aware of any such infringements, we will remove these contents immediately.

Liability for links

Our offer contains links to external websites of third parties, over whose contents we have no influence, and therefore we cannot assume any liability for these external contents. The respective provider or operator of the sites is always responsible for the contents of the linked sites. The linked pages were checked for possible legal violations at the time of linking. Illegal contents were not recognizable at the time of linking. However, a permanent control of the contents of the linked pages is not reasonable without concrete evidence of a violation of the law. If we become aware of any infringements, we will remove such links immediately.

Printed in Great Britain
by Amazon

28586564R00076